MINIMALISM FOR TEENS

How to use minimalism in your favor to build
the life you want and are happy with as a teen.

by Valentina Palermo V.

TABLE OF CONTENT

Introduction..5

What is Minimalism...7

How to be a Minimalist..9

Why Minimalism is Beneficial for Teens............................14

Learn to be Away From Your Phone.................................22

What to do if Your Family and Friends Don't Support You.....27

Why Minimalism will Make you a Better Student and Friend..31

Minimalist Living...33

What to do With your New Found Time............................39

How to Make Money as a Teenager.................................45

How to be Fashionable with a Minimalist Wardrobe............50

Make Your Time More Efficient.......................................54

Conclusion...57

INTRODUCTION

If you had to reduce everything you own to just a few items, what would you keep? If you had to live one year with just these items, which ones would you choose? This is an incredibly hard question, specially if you're not a minimalist as you're not aware of how many items you actually own and which ones you actually use.

You have probably heard about minimalism online or at least read about it a few times and it probably caught your attention or you wouldn't be reading this book. We're going to go through what is minimalism as well as how you can live a minimalist life.

People all over the world are starting to recognize that owning more things doesn't actually add what the media portrays. People are beginning to notice that the accumulation of things will not actually help them achieve anything and definitely won't make them happy. What actually makes life worth living is the experiences you have and the people you connect with. Nothing would be worse than realizing at the end of your life that you wasted every moment getting things that didn't matter to impress people you didn't even like and didn't make any deep connections with those who did or that you didn't travel as much as you wanted.

Excess stuff gets in the way of being able to live the life of freedom that you want. When you come to this realization is when you start getting rid of that which you don't need. It makes it a lot easier. Are there any material belongings holding you back? Think about it for a second and get rid of them if possible. Start living the life you want to live.

Living minimally is about appreciating the smell of your coffee in the morning without worrying about that which doesn't matter or the things you can't control. Or enjoying the view from your window without stressing about everything you need to do tomorrow. There are a few activities which you can do in order to live a happier life that have nothing to do with material possessions.

Minimalism will set you free because you will find out what is it that you really want so that you wont be pursuing the life you're "supposed to live" but rather the life you want. People seem to expect you to go to college, get a degree, get married, buy a house and then have children. If you want to do this then by all means go ahead, but if you feel there's something else you want to do or another path you want to explore then follow your heart and do so. Being aware of this reality while still being a teenager is one of the biggest advantages you can have. With minimalism you won't fear the opinions of others because you will know that what you're doing is the right thing to do. Most people waste their life pursuing the wrong things and become aware when it's too late.

WHAT IS MINIMALISM

Minimalism is living with enough items to maximize your happiness and wellbeing. While the concept of enough varies from person to person, it will most likely surprise you how little we actually need to live and be happy. Minimalism for you might mean owning only a few items while for others it might mean owning a lot more but still mindfully keeping only that which makes them happy and is useful.

Minimalism overall is about learning to be happy with less. It is about being free from the chains of objects and debt. People nowadays try to fill the emptiness with things, when in reality that's not the correct way to do so since it doesn't last. The happiness derived from objects fades away eventually, sometimes even a few hours after purchasing the item. In order to acquire these things, people sometimes go into debt to be able to afford them or to afford a lifestyle that's more expensive than what they earn. There's no way to justify this, as it will only lead to problems and stress.

Minimalism is about not letting yourself be distracted by things, which aren't the answer to a happy life. Happiness comes from experiences and becoming better everyday. A better person, a better friend, a better daughter, just strive to be better than yesterday and you will end up being a fantastic person. This doesn't mean you have to get rid of everything you own, just make sure that what you keep are things which make you feel happy.

Things take a lot from you even if you don't notice. It takes time to clean them and to keep them in a good state, it also takes time to organize them. It takes space to keep them and money to buy them. Having things is not "free", everything comes at some sort of cost. Whether it is space, time, money or all of them.

Minimalism will teach you to value peace and live in the moment. At the same time it will allow you to know yourself better, because once you reduce the noise around you the only thing left is to spend time with yourself.

HOW TO BE A MINIMALIST

There's no right or wrong answer as to what it takes to be a minimalist, it is just about having enough. Some minimalists like to live with almost no possessions while some do enjoy having a car and a house. It all depends on what you want and what makes you happy. Do not let others bring you down because of where you're in your minimalist journey. It is a journey after all and happiness is a choice. There isn't even a concrete definition of what minimalism is so don't let people tell you you're not a minimalist just because you don't live in an RV with 5 shirts and one pair of shoes. In fact, the only definition of minimalism which you will find is the one defining the art movement. So don't worry and take as much time as you want in your journey towards minimalism. And even if you decide you don't want to continue being a minimalist along the way I hope you did enjoy the time you spent following the minimalism principles and that you learned something valuable.

While you don't particularly need to just have 40 items to be a minimalist, you will see that when you adopt this lifestyle you'll find yourself wanting less things than you did before. The answer to the question of how you can be a minimalist is quite simple, get rid of the excess stuff. Take the first step, you will know when you've reached the ideal amount of things. One might think that the more we get rid of, the more were going to need and try to acquire back but in reality, it's the other way around. The less we have, the less we realize we need. So even if you minimize your items on the first round of decluttering, you're going to end up minimizing even more over time. When you start minimizing and actually start to see the benefits you will realize that what you originally wanted isn't what you want anymore. Same goes with the goals you set to yourself. Just like the items you own, these goals don't need to be static, there's no reason to be rigid as it is your life you're shaping at this moment. Just remember the decisions you take today can affect how you live tomorrow and you can't undo what you do. Think before you speak and before you act, because there's no undo button in real life. Ask yourself if what you're about to say is aligned with the person you are and who you want to be. If the answer is no then think about it for a bit before acting on impulse. Do not let feelings or emotions control you, if you feel like you're going to do something you might regret it is always best to get yourself out of that situation before it's too late. You can always come back later with a fresher and rational view of the situation.

Now it is time to get rid of the things you don't need. You can start anywhere you feel the most comfortable getting rid of stuff because there's less emotional attachment or for any other reason. Go through the different areas and categories of your items and concentrate on one at a time. Maybe it is easier to go through your school items from previous years and start throwing those away rather than trying to go through clothes that are filled with memories. This is completely your choice though, and the important thing is that you start.

In order to be a minimalist, it is essential that you find your core, these are the principles which will guide your life. People change over time but usually their values remain similar unless you allow them to change. This applies to your items as well, find which are your core items that you want to keep no matter what and then build around that. However, make sure not to add to much or you could lose sight of your "core".

Once you get rid of everything that's not needed, it is time to make sure you do not fill up that space again. Before buying anything, think about it for a few days. This way you will discard everything that you would have bought on impulse. It will also make you even more excited to get it if you wait a little longer. If you're tempted to buy it immediately, try asking yourself if you would replace something you already own in order to buy this thing and if it's worth the time invested in getting the money to afford it. If you're working, you're probably making around $10 per hour, so if you want a $50 shirt think of it in terms of hours worked. Is this shirt worth 5 hours of your time? Think of the value of money in other ways, what else could you do with those $50 you're about to spend? Maybe go out 10 times with your friends for a coffee or a snack.

Quality over quantity is the golden rule of minimalism. You want fewer things that are going to last you for years to come. Yes, this might be a bit more expensive than having lower quality ones but they'll pay for themselves over time.

My coach had a Louis Vuitton handbag that belonged to her grandma. This is what I mean with quality, this handbag could easily be 40 years old and it had been passed through 3 generations and it was still going strong. How many other handbags could you say can survive the test of time? Even if it had lasted 10 years that's still a lot of time for most items. Perhaps this isn't as common in clothes but think about the future. Consider if what you're getting is going to last you for at least a while.

I personally became a minimalism because I realized that I didn't need as many things as I had. And that I would be happier if I had less since I rarely even used most of the items. I'm one of those people who wanted to get rid of all the school material the day school ended since I saw no future use for it. Of course, my mom didn't let me because she thought it might be useful the next year. But the reality is, it rarely was. I also always had a pretty reduced wardrobe and have been wearing basically only black clothes since I was 13. Everyone said it was a phase... it wasn't. I still pretty much only own and wear black clothes. Black is my favorite color and it makes me happy to wear it.

In order to be a minimalist you're going to have a reason to do so. Why do you want to be a minimalist? Why do you think you will achieve with this journey? What do you love about minimalism from what you've seen so far? Definitely what I love the most is the freedom it gives me in many areas of my life. It's taught me how little we actually need to be happy and what really matters. I love that I could move anywhere at anytime without having to worry about my stuff, as I know things can be replaced. I love that it taught me what really matters and that I should be grateful for being where I am and surrounded by people who I love and admire. Another thing I love is that I could travel anywhere with just a carry on, knowing that's all I need and probably I'm carrying even more than that.

There's a rule I use before I buy anything and it is to ask myself if that item is going to make my life better. Do I need it or do I just want it? Minimalism is about having enough, which is a concept a lot of people find hard to embrace. We have been trained to want more and more, a desire that can never be satisfied. This is okay if your goal is to continue improving with self development each day but not when it comes to material things. Soon you will have one or two storage units to keep stuff that you don't even remember you bought. Sadly, we also tend to compete and compare ourselves with other people when in reality we should be striving to be the best version of ourselves. There are people whose identities are attached and defined by their possessions. So when they get rid of those they feel lost. If this is you, take the time to discover who you are, regardless of what you own.

WHY MINIMALISM IS BENEFICIAL FOR TEENS

Teens face a world full of distractions and decreasing attention spans, adopting minimalism helps you concentrate in those things that really matter rather than getting lost in everything that doesn't. In order to find those things, connections and activities that matter it is essential to take time to analyze what you normally do in a day and which ones of those activities, items or connections are important and helpful to you and which ones of those you enjoy.

Minimalism will help you in countless ways, here I have included a few which I consider the most beneficial.

Identify what's really important:
There are different types of activities. Those that matter and those that don't and those that make you happy and those that don't. You should focus on dedicating your time to those activities which make you happy and matter, even though there are some things you'll have to do (such as math homework) which are important even though you don't particularly like doing them. Make a list of your priorities and promise yourself you'll work on them.

Gain time:
You now know which activities are important and what you need to do. The easiest way to gain time is to eliminate those activities that don't matter and that aren't making you happy. However if you have a deadline to hit, you might have to

reduce the amount of time you spend on those that aren't important, even if they make you happy. Activities like this include watching videos on youtube or reading fiction books.

Set goals:
Setting goals is extremely important in any stage of life. This will help you get a clearer vision of where you want to go. Get a productivity planner. I have one which you can get **here** in which I worked for months to develop and find which areas were the best ones to include, if you are not interested in a printed productivity planner you can just spend $3 on a notebook and write your to do list and long term goals every single day. As long as you're consistent you will most likely achieve them.

Get rid of everything which is not useful or making you happy:
Why hold on to things you don't enjoy anymore? If they're not going to be useful to you in the future, get rid of them. These items are robbing you of your space and time, do not hold on to them just because you're too lazy to get them out of your life.

Reduce stress:
Studying and going through school is very stressful because you feel like you have to do a lot of homework but there's also the pressure to be social and attend parties and events. Being aware of how much time you actually have in a day and being able to organize it so that you can fit all the important activities is one of the skills you usually learn by being a minimalist.

Improve your diet and food choices:
Many minimalists become vegans or vegetarians, while diet is completely your choice, it would be very beneficial for your body if you aimed to eat more healthily. This means more fruits and veggies and less processed and fast foods. If time is an issue for you, you can leave your meals prepared the night before or even try meal prepping. This way you will have complete control over what you eat and you can make sure that most of the things you are consuming are actually healthy. Combined with exercise, this is one of the best things you can do to feel better and it's going to mark a huge difference in the long term as well.

Get to know yourself better:
Doing activities alone might sound like the weirdest advice ever. But it actually makes you spend time with yourself under a different setting. Also, if you go out to have a coffee or lunch by yourself, try not to use your phone. Use this time to think about how you're feeling and address the thoughts that come into your mind.

Become more aware of the information you're exposed to:
Pay attention to the type of information you're letting get to you. Watching the news or reading the newspaper can have negative effects on you as it is filled with negativity because that's what sells. If there's something that's important enough you can make sure it will get to you some way or the other. Your parents, friends or teachers will be talking about it, but this is the thing. It will have to filter through other people who are actively listening to news or reading the newspaper and you get to get informed by them rather than having to process all the other information. You can also use this opportunity to start a conversation and make more friends. If someone starts

talking about a recent event, you can ask them to tell you more.

Realize when you're not okay:
Do not let depression and anxiety get the best of you. Go to a psychologist to talk about your problems and solve them if you need to. Happiness is a choice for which you have to work towards everyday but it is worth it. Overtime it becomes easier to do so. Depression is like a hole, the more you think about it, the more you feel sorry for yourself, the deeper your hole becomes and the harder it is to come out. Avoid things or people than make you sad or that give you anxiety. Do not let anyone bring you down, you're a valuable person with an incredible potential that only you can let shine to the world. Anyone who tells you otherwise is lying. I believe in you and I know you can do great things in this world. You don't need anyone's permission to become your best self. Even bad moments come to an end. You need to realize you are not a victim of circumstance, everything that happens to you is because you either let it happen or you put yourself in a position that allowed it to happen. This might sound harsh but it also helps you realize that you can make things happen to get you out of that position and into whatever it is you want to be. You are in control of your life. You decide who you want to become.

Save money:
Saving money naturally happens when you start living minimally. Now when you see something you want, ask yourself if that item is going to improve your life in the long term or if it would be better to not spend money on it. There's a trick to make items less desirable and that is to think in terms of hours that you had to work in order to be able to buy it. If

you're eyeing a $250 pair of jeans and you make $14 per hour, that pair of jeans would cost you almost 18 hours of your life. Suddenly, it's not so appealing as it was 2 minutes ago.

Save time:
Buying less things means spending less which means you can work fewer hours if you want or keep working the same and save a lot of money which you can then invest. On top of buying less items, you also get rid of quite a lot of them so you have less stuff that needs to be cleaned and organized and you spend less time looking for the things you need as they all have their rightful place in your space.

Prevent you from going into debt:
The current American mindset of "get it now, pay later" has put many of us in debt. I've been in debt and let me tell you: it isn't fun at all. This is a difficult hole to crawl out of because the interest charges keep adding up. The cost of instant gratification ends up being a lot higher than ever imagined, specially if you don't know how to handle debt correctly. Since you're still a teen, you're most likely not in debt. Take advantage of that and try not to go into debt to finance something you don't need.

Peace of mind:
Since you're a minimalist, you're not really comparing what you have to what everyone else has. You are happy with the items you own because you don't need more than that and you know that when you do want something it is because it's going to add to your life. You're at peace because you're not competing a race that can't be won.

Be free:
Imagine you want to sail around the world but your boat is tied to an anchor and that anchor is all your possessions. The more you have, the more difficult it is to go anywhere. Owning too many things can be a great burden. The fewer things you have, the freer you will be to travel and move anywhere to live the life you want. Even when going to school, you will be free from carrying too many books and things and just take what's necessary.

Start a conversation about minimalism with anyone:
Odds are that if you're not someone who was brought up in a minimalist household you now have a new topic to talk to your family and friends about. You can even start a blog or social media account to document your progress and experiences with minimalism.

Get more space:
Your room will look bigger now that it's not filled with stuff. You will also have more space to do whatever you want to do such as practice yoga or dance. It will also look a lot cleaner now that there aren't any things on the floor or misplaced or even crawling out of a filled-beyong-capacity closet. You can also tailor your room to your needs. Once you start getting rid of things you figure out what is it that you actually use and helps you live a simpler life. Find your equilibrium and make sure to enjoy and appreciate every single one of the items you own.

Realize you can change your life because you are in control:
If you don't like the place you're at now you can change it. It is a lot more powerful to be in a situation which you hate than in a comfortable situation because this is going to be the

motivator that's eventually going to push you to move and change, to make your situation better and to put conscious effort every single day into changing it.

Be happier:
Most importantly, minimalism will help you to be happy. Focus on creating your own happiness, it all starts with the simple choice to just be happy.

We tend to adapt to any situation we go through so as you continue to grow and become better and happier with your life, just make sure to turn back every once in a while and be thankful and admire what you have achieved. Because it is necessary to remember where we come from and where we're going. Adaptation happens with good things, we eventually get used to them so that we're not always going to be excited about them. A simple example of this is when you get a new phone, at first you're super excited to use it and find out what it can do that your previous phone couldn't, but as time goes by and it become the usual, you don't continue to get the same excitement. Minimalism is about realizing you're good right now with what you have and where you are. Knowing that you could live with less with no problem as you made yourself rich by not needing much, so that everything extra that you acquire is actually a win. Our expectations will continue to go up and the best is to continue getting better, even if we only aim to be 1% better than the day before. As human beings we search for growth, this is why we need to become better each day. Even such a small change will lead to impressive results over time, believe me. Commit yourself to mastering abilities. You're going to learn a lot at the start but then it's going to be a small increase in abilities rather than the massive change you saw at the start. It might be hard to appreciate as you might've gotten used to such huge changes but once you approach that level, if you keep going you will get to results only a few people reach since not many have got one of the most important skills to have, persistence.

You need to be careful not to adapt to something which is not making your life better. As the same effect can happen in this scenario. You start getting used to laziness or any other behavior like that and before you know it, it has become the norm. It becomes normal to skip school or copy a homework, even if this was an awful thing to do a few months ago. Focus on creating small but powerful habits that will help you become better each day rather than routines that are hard to follow as these are easy to get out of and do not let yourself fall into the trap of "just this one time" because next time you do it, the bar will be set further away. When you set good habits you will naturally do what you need to do. Although this requires training too, once you form the habits you want, you'll continue to incorporate them in your life for years to come.

LEARN TO BE AWAY FROM YOUR PHONE

If you want to be a minimalist you need to get away from your phone. It is honestly an addiction for most people nowadays. Minimalism values freedom, and it seems phones are keeping us hostage by making us live in an alternative reality we can only see through the screen. Live in the now and learn to appreciate it, don't let yourself get lost into that world when you have another one right in front of you that's actually happening live. Your phone should help you in living a better life and not do the opposite. It is an amazing tool to communicate with those who are far away but don't let that affect the time you spend with people who are literally in front of you. If you're having dinner with your family or significant other, pay attention to them. You can check your phone later and if it's urgent then they will find a way to contact you. Turn off notifications every once in a while, even if its while you sleep or meditate. And don't look at your phone first thing in the morning. Develop a morning routine which will set you up for success everyday from the start. How often do you even check your phone? It's not like the world will stop if you don't answer to the gossip on the WhatsApp group.

Don't be a slave to your phone. Constantly checking your phone distracts you from your other activities. Think about how much faster you'd finish your tasks if you weren't switching from reading to your phone back and forth in the hour you spend reading. It is also naturally extremely distracting and it can trap you for hours, it seems that from the moment you unlock your phone for something, you end up being absorbed in a world of everything. Or if you open instagram or twitter one could spend hours just scrolling down. It is addictive, but most importantly it is time consuming. Think about all the other activities you could be spending time in, resting included.

There are a few things you can do in order to take back the power from your phone back to you. Turn off notifications unless they're absolutely necessary. You don't need notifications from social media or games. Although it makes sense to keep the messages, calls and email on. You can even tell people that if it's urgent that they can call you instead of messaging. There are many successful people who do not check their phones very often. This trains people in a way in which if there's a problem that needs to be solved immediately then they need to find a way to solve it because the boss is not going to be available until it is too late. Your time is extremely valuable, don't give it to anybody who wants it just because they're messaging you. Choose who you want to give it to and only when you want to give it.

If you believe you have an obsession with your phone there are books that you can read and even videos on youtube about how to stop your obsession. If you can't even go to the kitchen without your phone because you're feeling anxious then I would suggest you reevaluate your situation as you might have a problem you haven't realized you have.Aim to feel uncomfortable at times, because when you feel uncomfortable or scared it means you're doing something you wouldn't normally do and it's probably going to help you grow. It is part of that obsession with our phones and being connected which makes us feel unhappy with our lives.

Because we're looking at everything other people have and all the new items they get and they like to show it off on their social media. And it creates a scarcity in us, as if we needed to have and get everything our friends acquire when it's not that way at all. Stop comparing yourself to others, we all have different needs. Remember we usually only post the good things on social media and those things which we want the world to see. It is extremely uncommon for someone to post about something they're going through because we prefer to keep that private. So don't think everyone's life is perfect just because they show it like that. Life has its ups and downs, doesn't matter who you are or where you live. So allow yourself to go through those days in which you just feel sad and allow yourself to feel that sadness for a day, but then it is time to get up again and live life how were supposed to, by being content.

If you're going to have social media, try to make it enjoyable instead of a burden. Follow people which make you happy and who upload positive or educational posts. Or if you're going to follow people who have a lot of money, don't just follow those who only upload pictures of their Lamborghinis, follow those who upload pictures of their Lamborghinis but also tell you how they did it and what they're doing at the moment. Those who share their story because then you understand that they weren't just born in that situation, they worked hard to get to where they are and they actually earned all those luxury cars and million dollar properties. There's no such thing as get rich easy but there is a way to get rich quick if you know how to do it and what path to follow. Also be careful of those who sell you one way of getting rich quick or who try to give you advice on how to achieve something when they're not there yet. The best way to show that your teachings work is to demonstrate it in how you live.

There's also an obsession with multitasking caused in part by having our phones with us at all times. You don't realize you have an obsession until you detox from it. This obsession isn't seen as severe because of how common it is, everybody is using their phones at all times anyways. Did you know that your brain actually needs to "disconnect" in order to switch between activities. So when you're doing something and turn to check your phone because a new notification came in, you're breaking the flow you had and it's going to take you longer to get back into the previous activity, whatever it might have been. Even if turning for a few seconds to check your phone might seem like a harmless thing to do, you lose time and momentum every single time you switch activities. This time ends up adding up and making the tasks longer than they originally needed to be. Turn off notifications and delete the apps which are distracting you.

Find something to replace it. Now that you're making a conscious effort to not spend your life looking at your phone you will need something else to fill your time with. If you have more free time you will end up in the same activities if you do not replace it with something else. This can be anything you want, better if it is something useful. Get a notebook to write down what you're thinking and new ideas. A book you want to read and from which you want to learn something. Or just learn to be conscious of what thoughts are going through your mind.

Try going out without your phone or spend time without using your phone. The goal is that you spend time with the most important person, yourself. When was the last time you talked to yourself and evaluated your feelings and thoughts on a deeper level? Minimalism, since it reduces the noise around you, will make you get to know yourself better. Learn how to be alone with your thoughts and appreciate them as they could reveal patterns or feelings you weren't aware of but that might be affecting your life. If you want you can take a notebook and a pen to write any thoughts or ideas you have while you're out. Who knows, you might even end up writing a short story or the start of the book you've been postponing.

WHAT TO DO IF YOUR FAMILY AND FRIENDS DON'T SUPPORT YOU

Sadly, this isn't uncommon and you might face a lot of resistance if you want to be different, even if it's to become happier. Not everyone is going to support your transition to minimalism, specially because it is not what we are used to in society. Society itself places a huge influence on us as individuals and deters more people from becoming minimalists. We are naturally competitive, starting from our homes, to schools and even the workplace. Competition can be good but it's the extent at which it is pushed that makes it negative. People are sacrificing their health and sometimes even their lives in order to keep up with the latest trends and the lifestyle that the people close to them are living. So when these people start seeing that you are going another way that's not the designated path you'll experience resistance. The degree to which you experience said resistance will vary depending on the type of people you associate with, it can go from mild to extreme. You can try to explain this new lifestyle and most will not understand but just remember if you walk the walk you don't need to talk the talk. Let the happier you be the proof that you don't need more. It is not what you own but what you do with your life that matters. Find happiness in the goals that you achieve and not in the stuff you buy or the money you make. It is true that money won't make you happy but it's a lot more enjoyable to have money as it gives you freedom. Money is a tool, you decide how to use it. Strive to be happy now, there's no reason to wait to be happy. When the time comes that money arrives because of the value you provide to society, you will continue to be happy and pursue even more goals of yours. Never stop growing.

Don't try to force this lifestyle on to them, you are free to choose how you want to live and so are they. If they don't want to reduce the items they own, that is okay. The best you can do is to set an example with how you live your life so that they ask you what your secret to being happy is. Respects other's decisions to not be a minimalist as well as their items. Even if you see some of their things are actually damaging them, it is their decision to change it or not. Unfortunately even if they can't see how much it's affecting them it is not your job or decision to take it away from them. Everyone's journey is different and everyone is free to choose their own path.

Be intentional about what you acquire and how you spend your time. This includes the types of people you spend your time with. Be conscious about where you get the items you need and what your impact in this world is. Be kind to others and try to make friends and leave a positive image on those you meet. Because people will forget everything except how you made them feel.

You do not need to go to anything you don't want to, even if you think you're going to lose friends for it. Do not spend your time on activities you do not want to do. If your friends are pressuring you to go to a party, you don't have to say yes if you don't want to go. Just as you accept their decision to do whatever they want with their time and money you need to make them respect your own decisions and stand your ground. The cost of getting into alcohol consumption when you're young could end up costing you a lot more. It is not worth it and you do not need it to have a good time.

You might lose friends who don't want to accept your new minimalism trends since your priorities will shift from buying think that you like to only buying things that you actually need as well, so you'll notice yourself become pickier about what you bring into your life. Being pickier about things will also make you become pickier about activities and people. You'll find yourself no longer participating in activities which don't bring you joy or spending time with people who drain you rather than making you happy. You won't want to clutter your limited and organized space so you'll only get things that fit in every sense of the word and also, that you love.

Minimalism is viewed negatively by some individuals, calling minimalists cheap or crazy, believing we don't spend because we are stingy and thinking we aren't generous. Don't mind the haters. There's nothing wrong with staying liquid, specially in an economy that's coming out of a crisis and could go into another one at any time. Just because you have money doesn't mean you should be spending all of it. Have you seen the statistics of how much the average American has in savings? Most couldn't even cover a $1,000 emergency. This is something super scary if you think about it. Why would a person with no savings go spend $50 dollars on a Friday night? So don't let their negative opinions get to you, you know yourself better than anyone as if you don't consider yourself stingy then you most likely aren't.

As with everything, there are some cons that come with minimalism and one of them is precisely that not everybody will understand what you're doing. These are minor things which can present issues at the start but tend to be based of misinformation or judgement from people who don't understand the lifestyle. That's okay as we aren't all meant to live the same way and enjoy the same things.

If you're making a sacrifice to do something that's going to benefit you in the long run then if someone tells you that you're not doing the right thing it is because they probably haven't achieved much personally.

WHY MINIMALISM WILL MAKE YOU A BETTER STUDENT AND FRIEND

It is no secret that minimalism will free up your time since it is about freeing your life from distractions. There's a huge part of minimalism that focuses on eliminating time wasting activities and helping you ace through those which are important for your future such as school work.

But minimalism doesn't concentrate only on things and activities, it also helps you with the relationships with friends and family. It is no secret that we sometimes hold on to relationships which aren't good for us. Just like things that would weight you down if you were carrying them on your bag, these toxic relationships drain our energy and happiness. Sometimes it is better to say goodbye or to reduce the time you spend with these people. However, it will also help you realize which friendships are worth the time investment and will motivate you to continue nurture them, making you a better friend.

There's a cost for everything. Even if this cost is not measured in terms of money, it can be measured in terms of time. If you go out one night to party, you're not only spending money on food and drinks, you're also spending time there which you could be using to do any other activity. On top of that, if you're up until late that night, then at least half of the day after is going to be lost. If it were a school night then you'd have lost the classes you had in which you couldn't pay attention because you were almost falling asleep. Education isn't cheap, one time I calculated the cost of skipping one class at university, and take into consideration the university I went to wasn't as expensive, well, it was $15 per class. If you missed a day that meant you basically threw $60 into the trash.

By realizing how expensive it is to actually study whether it is in monetary or time terms, you will focus your best on finishing your homework and degree in the smallest amount of time possible, making your time spent more efficient and also dedicating yourself completely to study if that's what you set yourself to do.

MINIMALIST LIVING

There are a few activities which minimalists do in a different way because of the principles of minimalism. Here are some of them:

DECORATION

Since you're a teenager you probably still don't have a house of your own or still live with your parents so you can't really change as much as you would like to. Believe me, I've been there. There's nothing wrong with that. Even if you can't change the decoration of the whole house, you probably have a room to yourself which you can decorate how you want to. It is important to follow your parent's rules if this isn't your house but if you would like to make significant changes to your room such as paint the walls you should ask first.

You've probably seen those people on Instagram whose house and aesthetic is black, white and grey. You don't necessarily need to decorate your room this way unless you want to. The point here is that you should aim to decorate your space in a way that brings you peace and that doesn't distract you. Try to minimize the things you keep in plain sight and declutter your space. Clean your room and remember to maintain your space clean and uncluttered at all times. If your room is messy there's a high chance your brain will be preoccupied with it as well. Your room is the place where you should be able to rest but at the same time somewhere in which you feel safe and comfortable.

For decoration, pick those things which are meaningful for you but also helpful. Something like a lamp is probably essential to keep if you want some reading light at night but also things like a poster of someone who inspires you or a picture with your friends would be an amazing touch. Something I would suggest you include is a motivation board, with pictures of your goals, it would be a great touch as it keeps you focused on your goals while motivating you to do better everyday. If you want to change your furniture, you can always ask your parents to help you get new ones or you can even paint your old furniture yourself if you can't afford to get new items at the moment but still would like to change your room considerably.

Have a place for each one of your items so that you always know where to find them and where to keep them. This will save you time if you're looking for something, even if you haven't used it in a while.

TRAVEL

Traveling when you are a minimalist is the simplest thing there could be. My father used to tell me that as long as I had my passport, money and the plane ticket everything else could be replaced or solved if I forgot it. Of course I don't travel with just those items but I do enjoy traveling light. Traveling while young is one of the best things you can do as it exposes you to other cultures and sights of the world you'd have never thought existed until you visit them. Even if you're traveling inside the country I can assure you you'll learn so much and see so many things that it will forever change your outlook on life and the world itself. I'm personally all for saving and investing and I think travel is one of the best things you can invest in. Yes, it might be considered as an expense but I see it in terms of knowledge. When you learn something, that is an investment because you're spending money on something you'll be able to apply later.

As a minimalist you don't need more than a carry on to travel, whether it is for two days or two months. You can basically wear the same clothes you wear while you're at home and do laundry every week or two weeks. Packing for two weeks is more than enough clothes for a longer trip. Just make sure you check the weather of the place you're going to visit as it's not nice to arrive somewhere where it's snowing and not having a proper coat. And yes, that has happened to me as well. But as you can see, I have survived everything I've gone through so I have faith you can do as well. Traveling also exercises your problem solving abilities, making you a faster thinker and exercising speed of implementation.

If you do not like traveling that's alright, although I strongly recommend it. Try visiting somewhere new every once in a while, even if it is the shop you've never been to that's close to your grandma's house. Everything is valid.

SOUVENIRS

If you want to remember your trip to Italy, it is a lot better to take pictures than to bring back a lot of stuff. Because stuff eventually gets ruined and tossed away. While pictures can be kept as files for a lifetime in your computer or somewhere else. Just make sure to have a backup for them in case you lose where you're storing them. You can also keep them in the cloud or in google drive. Pictures are worth a thousand words and they will help you remember a place or event better than any type of souvenir. Of course, if there's something irresistible like a sweater you would like to add to your collection then by all means do so, after all it's about keeping you happy. I rarely buy clothes but I had to get a sweater when I went to New York, now I wear it every time I can and it reminds me of a fantastic trip.

REDUCING WASTE

This lifestyle is practical. Do we really need everything we have? And do we only keep that which we truly need? Having repeated items is a waste of resources. One interesting concept you can see in more apartment buildings nowadays is the implementation of shared spaces such as gym, laundry room, office space and event areas. This saves space inside your own home as you can just go a few floors up to exercise and the cost of all common spaces is distributed between all residents. One interesting topic to think about is how we are impacting the earth by switching to this way of living. How many resources are we saving just by not throwing away half of our things every two years and then replacing them with more, entering a vicious cycle.

UNDERSTANDING HOW WE WORK

Think of a roller coaster. The top of the ride is the purchase, you feel ecstatic and can't wait to bring it home. Then it's all downhill. You come back and unpack it and it's suddenly not as amazing. You use it a couple of times and then forget about it until you find it while you're spring cleaning. Wouldn't it be a lot easier just not to buy it? When you're buying something, your body experiences the effect of endorphins, which decrease over time. This works just like a drug, which is why some people are addicted to shopping and justify irrational decisions just to keep buying stuff they don't need because it makes them feel good. Understand that this happens and that you can get the same effect from achieving goals so that you're motivated to do productive activities rather than going out shopping.

MINIMALIST SPENDING

How you decide to spend your money is your decision. Just think about the pros and cons of buying stuff before actually doing so. You will most likely find yourself spending less money once you become a minimalist since you will want less things and you'll also think about the true cost of each item rather than just seeing a number also referred to as price.

REWARD YOURSELF

Use going out as an activity to reward yourself, same with watching TV or movies. Rather than it being the normal activity to do after school, use it as a motivator and treat it as something special. When I go to the gym I reward myself with one hour or TV or anything else I would like to watch since it's time spent doing something productive nonetheless.

BEING MINDFUL OF WHAT'S HAPPENING

You won't be able to hide away from your problems when you're a minimalist by distracting yourself with activities such as cleaning the accumulated mess you've been meaning to clean for months as a way to not deal with your emotions or stress. This is a positive thing as you will have to resolve that which is bothering you such as the math final tomorrow rather than go through your book collection deciding which ones to donate. You might even find events that are bothering you which you weren't aware of before.

WHAT TO DO WITH YOUR NEW FOUND TIME

It doesn't make sense to find ways to free up your time if you're not going to use it for something productive or that will help you feel better or happier. So now that you have identified those activities you tend to do that aren't adding to your life, you can use the free time to do something else. It's important you start setting goals for yourself so that you can work towards them as time passes.

MEDITATE

Even if it's just about thinking about your day for a few minutes during the day, this will help you relax and have a different perspective on events. There are different types of meditation but you can basically use meditation to help you relax or to find a solution for a problem.

PRACTICE GRATITUDE

Practicing gratitude will help you be a happier person as it centers on everything you have rather on what you don't have. You can be grateful for anything. You have access to food, shelter, clothes and education. If you can't find anything to be grateful for, just be grateful for being alive. This is one of the most powerful things since as long as you're still alive, you can change anything you want. You can fix anything if you set your mind and energy to it. When I was 19 years old, one of my friends died of hypothermia, she was my age. I don't think I've ever felt as much pain as I felt that day when I found out but I think the worst part was that I knew I couldn't change anything about her death. But then I realized I could change myself and how I was living. Since then I decided I was going to aim to be the best person I possibly could as a way to honor her.

Again, instead of focusing on all that which you don't have, focus on everything you've been given. You are alive, you're healthy, you have a place to live and food to eat on a daily basis. Most people in the world don't have the same blessings you have. Take a moment of your day to practice gratefulness and write down one thing for which you're grateful for today.
If everything else fails, I always picture the worst case scenario and then I'm grateful for the position I'm in. It happens to a lot of people that they start thinking about everything that could go wrong and that generates anxiety. But if you picture the worst case scenario then you can start finding solutions that you could put into practice in case said scenario happened. Realizing that even the worst has a solution puts you back in control of your life, instead of taking the position of a victim.

EXERCISE

Exercise will help you a lot in every aspect of your life. It will help you feel better, relax, sleep better and even think faster since it increases the blood flow. Take care of your health, we don't really appreciate it until something happens to us. A strong body helps develop a strong mind. Being consistent is the only way you will get the results you want. Aim to be really good at something rather than just trying it out for 30 days and then switch to another thing. So if you start doing weights or yoga, just stay consistent and you will end up seeing the results very soon.

BE CONSISTENT

Make a commitment that you will dedicate at least 1 year to whatever activity you decide to do such as learning how to play the piano or starting a youtube channel. Trust the process, small improvements overtime are better than no improvements. Even if it feels like you're running in place, something is happening that's making you better each day.

SPEND MORE TIME WITH FAMILY AND FRIENDS

These are relationships in which you have to invest time in order to help them flourish. Make an effort to get along with your family and make time for your friends when they need you.

GET CREATIVE

Whatever it is you enjoy doing, you now have time to do so. You can paint, draw, dance or create anything else that goes through your mind. You can even do a business plan and operations flowchart for the business you want to create in the future. Being creative and making something from zero will help you be creative in other areas as well.

FIND A MENTOR

As a teen it is important to have someone you admire who you can talk to or at least get advice from. Look for a mentor, this person can be someone close to you or someone you can watch on the internet consistently whose values align with yours. We have the great advantage to live in a digital era in which you can have access to pretty much everyone over the internet. If you choose your mentor to be Tony Robbins you can just look for videos of him on youtube or even find interviews of him talking. There's enough material there to last you for months and there's always going to be more content coming.

EXPERIENCE MORE THINGS

Experiences are one of the most valuable things you can get. Because as knowledge, no one can take this away from you and they increase the baseline of your happiness as opposed to items with which you return to your original level of happiness. Experiences can be anything from going to the local coffee shop to traveling to the other side of the world. Even working as a nanny counts as an experience. Experiences last a lifetime and no one can take them away from you. So unless you have really bad memory or something happens they will remain with you. Aim to become a collector of experiences rather than a collector of items. They also add give you a new perspective. If you travel I can assure you that you'll go back to your country with at least one idea for a business or a book.

LEARN

Make time to read. Just because you're going to school doesn't mean you're going to get all the knowledge you need in order to be successful or to get where you want. School is about learning to learn and the things you learn there are pretty broad. But the magic about books is that you can just pick any topic and then read as many books as you want on that topic. Becoming an expert doesn't take that long if you put time and effort into it. It is still important to go to school because it also helps you develop in social situations and you do end up learning but it's on you if you want to learn about finance before graduating. This is something which I believe should be taught in schools but that might come with time. Same goes with topics such as minimalism, it is a niche topic which not all people are interested in, so I'm glad you're reading this book. The best way to make sure that you actually learned something is to produce the content yourself. After you read a book or while you're reading it, try to write down what you learn and how you can apply it to your life. Finding a use for what you've just learned will make it a lot easier for you to remember it and it will also develop the structure of your brain as the neuronal networks will grow and sometimes connect depending on what you're learning and how you're applying it.

LISTEN TO AUDIO BOOKS

Since you probably don't have to drive as you have access to the bus or some other sort of public transportation. Or even if you do have a car and drive to school or to the gym. Use this time to listen to your mentors or listen to audio books. You don't need to sit down for an hour to read a book on self development anymore, you can just download it and listen to it while you're in traffic or at the gym.

LIVE IN THE MOMENT

Living in the past causes depression and living in the future causes anxiety. Enjoy the moment you're living right now instead of wishing things were like they were before or worrying about events that will probably never happen. Enjoy the moment and admire what's going on around you.

SET GOALS AND WORK TOWARDS ACHIEVING THEM

We've talked about goal setting before. Your prefrontal cortex will actually thank you for setting goals and you will be a lot more likely to achieve them if you write them down and follow some guidelines about goal setting. Make them specific and set a designated deadline, then plan what you need to do each month, week and day in order to achieve them. Having goals will have you excited about the future and reaching the mini goals you set along the way will keep you motivated.

LEARN A NEW SKILL

Skills are an investment as they add value to you. What's the reason why some people get paid more than others? Simple, they have a more valuable skill set. People who go to college usually earn more than those who don't, and those who have work experience and a college degree can opt for a higher salary. The only reason why someone is making $10 per hour is because they haven't put in the work to increase the value of their time. Be careful though, as 10 years at a job doesn't mean you've become better at it, it usually means you've spent 10 years doing the same thing. Focus on learning something new every single day.

HOW TO MAKE MONEY AS A TEENAGER

Apart from school, teens usually spend a lot of their time watching Tv, Netflix or Youtube, or using Instagram and Snapchat. Feeling identified? To be fair, so did I, but what if instead of spending time doing that you could create a source of income that you can use to spend in whatever you like such like a trip outside the country or an item you've wanted for a long time?

Just because you are young doesn't mean you can't earn money. Thanks to all the internet platforms you now have access to many ways to make money. Instead of watching videos on Youtube you can now create your own content and share it with other people. You now have an advantage as you know what makes a good video, it's present in all of those videos which make you watch them until the end. Plus, the abilities you'll learn while doing so could be very helpful in the future as well. If you are underage, you can ask your parents for help or permission depending on the website's regulations and state laws.

How to make money as a minimalist is an easy question to answer and it doesn't have to get complicated just because of your age. Minimalism helps free your time, even if it is your free time after school. Time which you can make productive by creating a new source of income which could eventually end up being the main one. Making money is such a huge topic because usually it is your job which takes the most amount of your time. In order to leave your job you would either need to 1 reduce your expenses or 2 increase your income. Take advantage of being a teenager and not having to work yet in order to live comfortably without having to worry about having a job and performing well in it. In most cases, your parents are still paying for your education and living expenses.

WRITE A BOOK

One of the ways to make passive income while doing something you enjoy is to write a book. If you enjoy writing, like me, this won't feel tedious even if you're writing 4,000 per day as a way to challenge yourself. You can write fiction or non fiction but the best advice I can give you is to write about a topic you know well and find interesting. This brings me to the second way to make passive income online.

START A BLOG

Blogs can be an amazing way to connect with people with the same interests as you. If you decide to write about a topic which you're passionate about such as minimalism, your blog will most likely attract the attention of minimalists if you're creating value for them in the form of entertainment or education. This would cost around $120 for both the domain and the hosting and then you would have to produce the content yourself or hire a ghostwriter. There are plenty of websites that you can use to do this, I personally use Squarespace to host my blogs as I find it is a friendly platform to work with.

AMAZON FBA

You've probably seen people making a ton of money off of amazon FBA. There are Youtubers who started doing this while they were still teens and they're now making enough income to not have to work a traditional job. Aim to fulfill a need in a market that's not too saturated. Even though the investment needed to start selling on amazon FBA is not as high as the investment needed to start other businesses, it is still considerably higher than starting a blog or with amazon KDP. You are looking at $2,000 to $5,000 to start a business like this comfortably.

START A YOUTUBE CHANNEL

Another way of making money online is to start a YouTube channel. There are people who are better at talking than they are at writing and vice versa. The best part about starting a YouTube channel is that the abilities needed aren't that many and you can even film the videos with your phone, virtually anywhere in the world. And use editing programs which basically come with your computer. The cost to start with YouTube is basically zero as you can start by using what you already own. The highest cost would be the time you'll need to invest in learning how to edit a video so that you can upload a better version and also learn how to make thumbnails that catch the viewer's attention.

FREELANCE WEBSITES

Offering your skills on websites such as Fiverr or Upwork lets you share your talents with the world and the customers that hire you as a freelancer. While this is not passive income, you can use it to build your savings or to fund your passive income investments. If you have a valuable skill which you would like to share with the world, this is the way to do so. Maybe you're amazing at designing presentation cards or formatting ebooks, well this is one of the easiest way to find clients.

GET A PART TIME JOB

If you would prefer to work a part time job after school or during the summer, this is also a great idea. Working during the summer or in the afternoon will be beneficial for you since it teaches you about responsibility and the value of money. Earning your own money will make you conscious of how much time and energy it requires to actually acquire $100, rather than just getting it as a gift for your birthday or Christmas.

One of the biggest barriers teens have when doing pretty much anything is the lack of access to money and resources. A lot of employers (and even investors) will be hesitant to give you a job or an opportunity because of your age. Believe me, it has happened to me many times as well. The best way you can change their minds is by showing them you're capable and responsible.

Start saving when you're young. If you start saving now, you will be ahead of the thousands of Americans who do not have savings over $1,000. Take advantage of the fact that you still don't have any money responsibilities and save so that when you want to do something big, you have a way to finance it rather than having to go into debt to do so.

There's a process to everything. You need to understand that you can't grow a tree faster by planting more seeds, there are some things which take time and they're worth the time invested. As your abilities grow, so will your income sources.

The best type of income is passive income, which is the one that requires a big investment at the start but then it can maintain itself without you having to put time into it. The main requirement to earn passive income is to add value in a way which can continue to generate income without you being there rather than to be compensated for the time you put in. Let's say you start a Youtube channel and monetize it, you will continue to earn income as long as your video continues being relevant. If you work at a shop, you only get paid for the hours you work. Ultimately, it is your choice which route you want to follow. But whatever it is you're doing, just make sure you're contributing with something valuable. Always go forward and be resourceful. Everything is available if you know how to access it.

HOW TO BE FASHIONABLE WITH A MINIMALIST WARDROBE

Do you love everything you wear? Are you excited to get up in the morning and get dressed or are you dreading having to pick something out for that day? Or do you dread having to get up and choose something as you know it'll take you a good 10 minutes because nothing fits and nothing matches? Well, it is time to fix this.

There are countless advantages to owning a minimalist wardrobe, whether it is small in the amount of clothes you own or just very neutral in colors. The amount of time it will save you is life-changing as well as avoiding the frustration in the morning caused by not knowing what to wear. Paralysis by analysis is real, prevent yourself from self-sabotage by culling your wardrobe.

Having a reduced amount of clothes leaves you without much choice so that you have to make a decision faster and sticking to neutral colors makes it easier for you to match the pieces. This doesn't mean all of your clothes have to be grey, black and white but that would also be more efficient. Having less clothes than your friends does not mean that you have to sacrifice style or fashion, if anything it will make your wardrobe even more interesting since you will have a signature look that everyone recognizes that fits your personality perfectly. Your teens are the years in which you are discovering who you are and experimenting with different styles, although it is most likely that you have already found which clothes and colors you enjoy wearing more. Use this knowledge of yourself to start building the wardrobe of your dreams.

Okay, now it is time to go through your stuff. There are a few guidelines to follow if you want to make getting rid of stuff easier. If it is broken, falling apart or has a hole, throw it away. If you haven't worn it in over a year, throw it away. If it is an item you have to alter or fix but haven't brought yourself to do so, get rid of it unless you commit to getting it altered in the next 3 days. If it looks old in a bad way or outdated, get rid of it. If you don't like it, put it in the donating pile. If it does not fit you, throw it away. This applies if it is too big, too small or if the color or design just don't go well with you. It is time to say goodbye to those pieces which you wore when you were younger that no longer fit you whether it is because of the size or the style. The best items to keep are those in which you feel the most comfortable in and wear more often. Remember that when you donate your clothes you could be helping other people who actually need them, don't throw away items that could still be useful to someone else.

Once you've gone through all your stuff and donated the clothes you haven't used in a year that you keep telling yourself you will wear but never do it is time to address the problem of how they got into your closet in the first place. Because the only one who could've put those clothes there is you. There's no excuse because even if someone pressured you to buy a certain item, it was you who ultimately had to say yes, take it home and place it in your closet.

Why are you buying clothes you don't wear and you know you're not going to wear? Is it because you go shopping with someone who pushes you to buy stuff? Or do you convince yourself to buy it for whatever reason? Well, whatever it is, it is time to stop. There are some simple tricks to use if you want to make sure you really want to make the purchase.

One of the easiest ways to start and keep a minimalist wardrobe is to experiment with the capsule wardrobe. When doing a capsule wardrobe a lot of people like having different items as it will give them a lot more looks. You could create up to like 500 look combinations if you really try to optimize your pieces. Whether you get bored wearing the same thing everyday and prefer to take this approach or don't mind to have like 4 total outfit combinations is up to you. But going through this experience will definitely teach you a lot, even if you decide not to stick to having a capsule wardrobe after the season is over.

A capsule wardrobe is basically a wardrobe which has around 30 items and it revolves around a few high quality pieces that are going to last you for at least a season. The point of this is to reduce your items to only those which you need and it was originated because most people tend to wear just a few items of clothes, even when they own 100+ pieces. Find what your style is like by looking at the clothes that remain and that you wear most often. Your color palette should be pretty evident here as well.

There are a few basics to follow when building a capsule wardrobe to make it a lot easier. Stick to mostly neutral colors. Have a color palette consisting of three neutral colors (black, white, blue) and two accent colors (red, green). Take the season you're in in consideration so that you can have appropriate clothes for the weather. Have your capsule wardrobe be flexible enough to be able to go to work or a formal event as well as just spend a relaxing evening in your home. Build it around a few essential items such as a jacket, a few shirts, jeans or leggings and comfortable shoes. Document your process and feelings, you might discover something you weren't aware of once you're separated from your extra clothes. Make it fun, upload pictures to instagram or write about it.

Now it is time to start adding to your wardrobe. Make a list of everything you need such as a coat or a pair of shoes that you don't currently have. Be mindful of what you buy and don't get it unless you're 100% sure it is something you want in your wardrobe and that you are going to wear.

MAKE YOUR TIME MORE EFFICIENT

You probably have school work and other activities to complete if you're still a teen. While these activities might take up a big chunk of your time, it is still not as much time as what a full time job would take. Take advantage of the fact that you don't have to work yet and use your free time after school to do something productive that aligns with what you want to do.

There are a few steps to follow in order to use your time more efficiently:

- Make a list of the most important activities you do on a daily, weekly or monthly basis and try to make it as efficient as possible. Commit to spending a certain amount of time doing these and streamline the process as much as possible. Have you seen that McDonalds' kitchen is set a particular way so that every order can be fulfilled in less time? Well, the good news is that you can apply this to your own processes. Simple things like leaving your clothes ready the day before or putting everything you'll need in the morning in a single place will reduce the time you spend doing each activity.

- Spend time in activities that matter and that are going to produce the results. Plan your day so that you can do everything you set yourself to do and achieve maximum efficiency.

- Set goals in every aspect of your life such as academic or learning, work or money making, friendship and relationships, physical and health, etc.

- Be committed to your goals, if you're serious about doing something then do it. You'll waste more time switching from activity to activity than actually achieving your goals if you're dabbling. If you need to do so, have an accountability partner or make yourself accountable in your social media. If you're going to use it at least use it for something productive.

- You don't need to have an extremely strong reason or motivator to change for the best if you don't want to but it is important to have a reason why you're doing this. So that when times get difficult, you find a way to continue and push through.

- Look within you to find what is it that adds value to your life. Then dedicate more time to these activities.

- Don't worry about the future as you're the one who decides where you want to lead your life. Instead, create the future you want.

- Embrace uncertainty as it is part of everybody's life. You can't be 100% sure of everything all the time. Just prepare for the worst and expect the best.

- Last but not least, use your nerves to your favor. You can use all this energy in a positive way, it just depends on your thoughts. Think of the nerves as nerves from excitement. Use it to feel happier and excited about new activities, embrace the nerves.

It's up to you to make your time more efficient and make the most out of it. If you start laying down the foundation for your habits from this moment, you will have them all reinforced later in life, giving you a competitive advantage over everyone else.

CONCLUSION

Now that you have finished this book on minimalism, it is time to start applying it to your life. Declutter it from everything which isn't adding to it. Time is the most important and scarce of our resources, don't waste it by spending time in activities that don't matter or with people who aren't adding to your life. This includes irrelevant relationships and items which are holding you back instead of letting you be free.

There are three simple steps to keep you on track when you're a minimalist.

- The first one is to get rid of everything that you haven't used in a while (and don't plan to use soon) and that's not bringing you happiness.

- The second one is to only keep and acquire those items which are useful but at the same time bring you joy.

- And the third one is to not let clutter come back into your life.

There's no right or wrong way to be a minimalist, just stick to what works for you. Keep only the things that matter and that make you happy. Society tries to tell us to live a certain way but the best way is the one you choose yourself as only you know what you like and how you want your life to be.

There are many benefits to being a minimalist, some of there are to save time, money and energy by eliminating activities that aren't beneficial for you. Also, you will be able to travel a lot easier and to have a wardrobe full of pieces you enjoy wearing and which fit you perfectly.

Remember that just because you're a teen doesn't mean you can let that hold you back, on the contrary, you're at an advantage right now because you have more time than those who are already adults and working on a traditional job. Use your free time after school or university to start building a source of income, this can be as fast and easy as starting your Youtube channel or writing an ebook on a topic you enjoy. Don't compare yourself to people who already have millions of subscribers, everybody's journey is different and yours has just started. Instead, aim to be better than you were yesterday and you will end up even higher.

If someone gives you a hard time for being a minimalist or for trying to work on making your life better then that person doesn't want what's best for you and will most likely limit your growth on different areas, not just this one. Remind them that you're not trying to change them, you're just trying to improve yourself and if they do not understand or don't respect your decision, make a conscious decision to spend less time with them as they will hold you back from reaching your full potential.

Start your minimalism journey by decluttering as much or as little as you want, after all this is supposed to be enjoyable and some people take longer to realize what is it that really adds to their happiness. Keep only those things which you love, that are useful or that you need and don't let someone else tell you how to live your life as only you know what you want.

www.ingramcontent.com/pod-product-compliance
Lightning Source LLC
Chambersburg PA
CBHW070427240526
45472CB00020B/1509